STUDENT BOOK

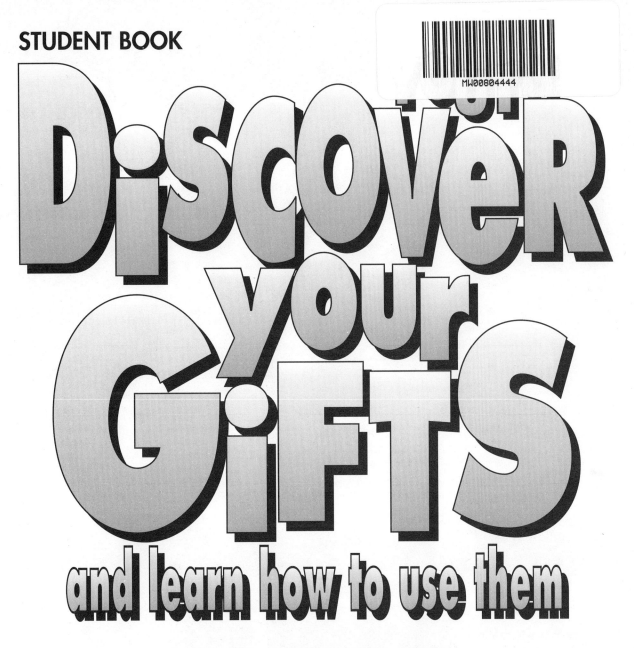

DiSCOVER YOUR GiFTS

and learn how to use them

RUTH VANDER ZEE

CRC Publications
Grand Rapids, Michigan

CRC Publications thanks Ruth Vander Zee for writing this
course. A teacher at Timothy Christian Middle School in
Chicago, Illinois, Vander Zee adapted part of her course from
the adult version of *Discover Your Gifts*, written by Alvin J.
Vander Griend. © 1996, CRC Publications.

Cover illustration: Todd Clary

10 9 8 7 6 5 4 3 2 1

Session 1
What Are Spiritual Gifts?

> Brothers and sisters, I want you to know about the gifts
> of the Holy Spirit. . . . There are different kinds of gifts. But they are all
> given by the same Spirit. There are different ways to serve. But they all come from the
> same Lord. There are different ways to work. But the same God makes it possible for all of
> us to have all those different things. The Holy Spirit is given to each of us in a special way:
> that is, for the good of all. . . . All of the gifts are produced by one and the same Spirit.
> He gives them to each person, just as he decides.
> (1 Corinthians 12:1, 4-7, 11, NIrV)

OK, so you know that spiritual gifts don't come on a UPS truck.
But where do they come from and what are they for? Try filling in this simple definition:

Spiritual gifts are various skills, attitudes, and abilities
given to each _____ by the one
_____ through the _____ _____
to be used for the spiritual _____ of _____.

👉 Why do you think the gifts are called "spiritual" gifts?

👉 Do you honestly believe the Spirit has given you one or more spiritual gifts?
Why or why not?

Session 1
Unwrapping the Gifts

Directions: For each gift that you've been assigned, first look up the biblical example of the gift in action. Then write a short sentence telling who used that gift and how. Next, give an example of how someone your age might use the gift for the benefit of others. The gift of "administration" has been done for you as an example.

Administration

The ability to organize and help people work together.

Biblical example (Acts 6:1-4):
The twelve disciples delegate responsibility for caring for the needy to seven deacons.

Current example:
Organizing our youth group into teams for preparing and serving a spaghetti supper to the congregation.

Discernment

The ability to tell if someone or something is right or wrong, real or fake.

Biblical example (Acts 8:14-21):
_____
_____

Current example:
_____
_____
_____

Creative Ability

The ability to use music, art, drama, writing, drawing, acting, dancing, and similar gifts in ways that are pleasing to God.

Biblical example (Acts 1:1):
_____
_____

Current example:
_____
_____
_____

Encouragement

The ability to use your words and actions to cheer people up, to motivate them to do something that's hard for them, to help them live in a way that's pleasing to God.

Biblical example (Mark 14:3-6):
_____
_____

Current example:
_____
_____
_____

Evangelism

The ability to tell others about Jesus' love for them in such a clear and understandable way that God is pleased.

Biblical example (Acts 8:26-31):

_____

_____

Current example:

_____

_____

_____

_____

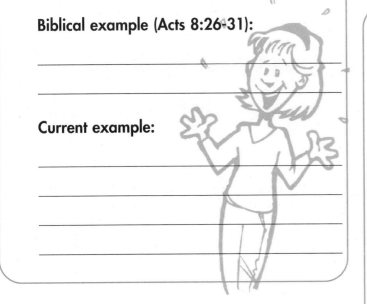

Giving

The ability to cheerfully and generously share our time, money, and possessions with those in need.

Biblical example (Luke 21:1-4):

_____

Current example:

_____

_____

_____

Faith

The ability to know for sure that God's promises are true and trustworthy, even when circumstances make others doubt the promises.

Biblical example (Acts 27:21-26):

_____

_____

Current example:

_____

_____

_____

_____

Hospitality

The ability to make persons of all ages feel "at home" and comfortable—especially persons who are guests or strangers.

Biblical example (Acts 16:14-15):

_____

_____

Current example:

_____

_____

_____

_____

Intercession

The ability to pray faithfully for others.

Biblical example (2 Tim. 1:1-3):

_____

_____

Current example:

_____

_____

_____

Mercy

The ability to feel the hurts of others and to help them cheerfully in meaningful ways.

Biblical example (Acts 9:23-28):

_____

_____

Current example:

_____

_____

_____

Leadership

The ability to take charge, to set an example for others, to serve others by helping them reach their goals.

Biblical example (Acts 1:15-16; 2:14):

_____

_____

Current example:

_____

_____

_____

_____

Prophecy

The ability to know God's Word and to talk boldly about important issues to those who don't understand or who need to be encouraged or convinced.

Biblical example (Acts 17:22-23):

_____

_____

Current example:

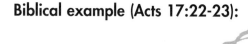

_____

_____

_____

_____

Service

The ability to help others in practical ways.

Biblical example (Acts 9:36):

_____

_____

Current example:

_____

_____

_____

_____

Teaching

The ability to clearly explain things about God and how God wants us to live.

Biblical example (Titus 2:1-2):

_____

_____

Current example:

_____

_____

_____

_____

The **SPIRITUAL GIFTS** ◀ • • • • • • • •

I think the Spirit may have given me are:

_____

_____

_____

_____

Session 1
Prayer Journal

Date of Request   **Request**   **God's Answer**

Date of Request   **Request**   **God's Answer**

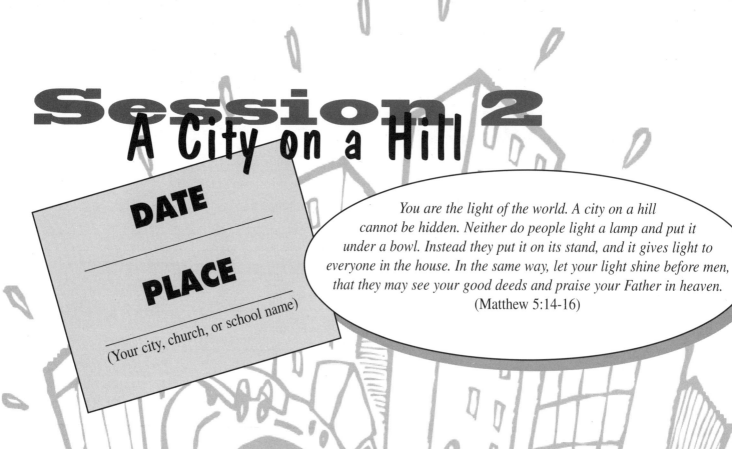

Session 2
A City on a Hill

DATE

PLACE

(Your city, church, or school name)

You are the light of the world. A city on a hill cannot be hidden. Neither do people light a lamp and put it under a bowl. Instead they put it on its stand, and it gives light to everyone in the house. In the same way, let your light shine before men, that they may see your good deeds and praise your Father in heaven.
(Matthew 5:14-16)

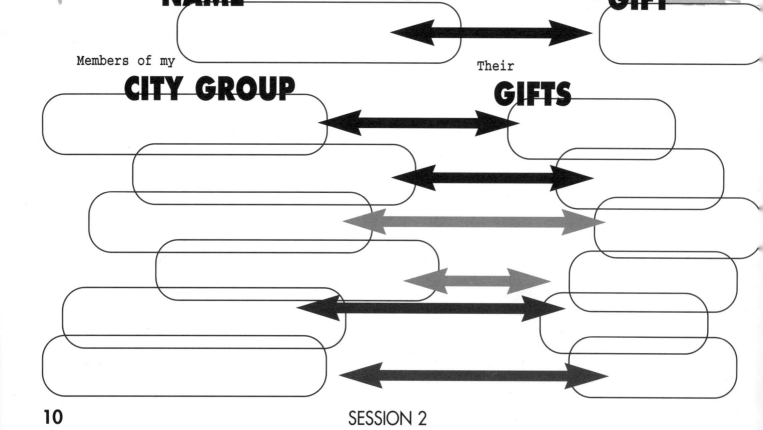

My
NAME

My
GIFT

Members of my
CITY GROUP

Their
GIFTS

Session 3
Tangram Teaser

Directions:
Cut out the pieces of this tangram. Then, as directed by your teacher, use the pieces to make pictures that represent various spiritual gifts.

Session 4
Celebrate!
YOU ARE GIFTED!

If you are a believer in Jesus Christ,
the Holy Spirit has given you spiritual gifts
so that you

- ☞ can serve others.
- ☞ can help the body of Christ be one body.
- ☞ can praise and glorify God.
- ☞ can (with others) grow into a mature Christian.

God has given you

WORKING GIFTS
These are gifts you are already using in some way.

WAITING GIFTS
These are gifts you've been given but haven't had an opportunity to use yet. Waiting gifts may later develop into working gifts.

The combination of gifts that God has given you is called your

GIFT MIX
Remember—when you use your spiritual gifts, you're doing God's work in the world!

Session 4
Completing the Questionnaire

In a few minutes you will be asked to complete a spiritual gifts questionnaire. The questionnaire will help you discover your gifts or affirm you in the gifts you already have.

While the questionnaire is as accurate as we can make it, it's not perfect. You may have more gifts than it suggests. Or it's possible that you may not have a gift that it says you have. Don't worry about that. This questionnaire is just a tool to help you discover more about yourself. As you live the Christian life, the gifts you've been given will become evident. Don't be disappointed, either, if the questionnaire suggests you don't have certain gifts that you really would like to have. Remember that God has gifted others in the body of Christ with the gifts that you may not have. No gift is unimportant; all gifts are necessary. Each person has his or her own unique gift mix. *Together,* we can help do God's work in the world.

Each statement in the questionnaire has five possible responses:

VERY LITTLE
means this statement is 0-20% true of you.

1

LITTLE
means this statement is 20-40% true of you.

2

SOME
means this statement is 40-60% true of you.

3

MUCH
means this statement is 60-80% true of you.

4

VERY MUCH
means this statement is 80-100% true of you.

5

- Read each statement.
- Decide to what extent the statement is true of you.
- Check the appropriate column.

Answer as accurately as you can (your first impression is probably your best answer—be honest with yourself). Don't worry if most of your marks are placed toward the right or toward the left. But try to avoid putting too many marks in the middle ("Some") column. You will find your own way to answer the questions.

The following is TRUE of me . . .

	Very Little (1)	Little (2)	Some (3)	Much (4)	Very Much (5)
1. When a group project is assigned at school, I like being in charge.	☐	☐	☐	☐	☐
2. I am good at one or more of the following activities: drama (acting), writing, art, music, creative dance, sewing, problem solving, finding new ways to do things.	☐	☐	☐	☐	☐
3. I know when people are saying things that aren't true about God or the Bible.	☐	☐	☐	☐	☐
4. I am often able to help people who are discouraged or who have a problem.	☐	☐	☐	☐	☐
5. I like to talk about Jesus with friends or with others who don't know him.	☐	☐	☐	☐	☐
6. When others are confused about a difficult situation, I seem to know what God would want me to do.	☐	☐	☐	☐	☐
7. When our church or school sponsors a project to help needy people, I bring food or give some of my time or money.	☐	☐	☐	☐	☐
8. When new kids join our class at school or at church, I help them feel comfortable.	☐	☐	☐	☐	☐
9. When others ask me to pray for them, I do—more than once.	☐	☐	☐	☐	☐
10. When I'm working in a small group, I help group members do their best.	☐	☐	☐	☐	☐
11. When someone is going through a hard time, I feel sorry for them and often help them in some way.	☐	☐	☐	☐	☐

	Very Little (1)	Little (2)	Some (3)	Much (4)	Very Much (5)
12. I am not afraid to talk to others about God when I feel there is a need.	☐	☐	☐	☐	☐
13. When a group is working on a project, I like to do "behind the scenes" jobs that help make the whole project successful.	☐	☐	☐	☐	☐
14. When someone, even a young child, has a question about God or the Bible, I often can explain things clearly enough to answer his or her question.	☐	☐	☐	☐	☐
15. I like to plan projects that a group at school or church might do.	☐	☐	☐	☐	☐
16. If given a chance, I would like to use my writing, drawing, musical, dramatic, or other artistic ability at school or church.	☐	☐	☐	☐	☐
17. When someone says something about God or the Bible that I don't believe is true, I feel very uneasy.	☐	☐	☐	☐	☐
18. I would like to help people at church or school who are going through a hard time.	☐	☐	☐	☐	☐
19. If given the chance, I would like to talk to people who don't know Jesus.	☐	☐	☐	☐	☐
20. When I have a problem, I don't get too upset because it always seems that God helps me through it.	☐	☐	☐	☐	☐
21. When my school has a project to help people who are poor or hungry, or if someone needs help, I often feel that I would like to help them.	☐	☐	☐	☐	☐
22. When someone new comes to my school or church, I would like to help them feel welcome.	☐	☐	☐	☐	☐
23. When someone has a prayer request, I try to remember to pray for him or her.	☐	☐	☐	☐	☐

24. The next time my school or church has a special project, I would like to help lead the group working on the project from start to finish.   ☐ ☐ ☐ ☐ ☐

25. When I see someone with a disability, I would like to help them in a meaningful way.   ☐ ☐ ☐ ☐ ☐

26. I believe that the Bible talks a lot about everyday situations. When an issue comes up in class, I feel I should say what the Bible teaches about that issue.   ☐ ☐ ☐ ☐ ☐

27. I can tell when others need help, and I would like to help them in any way I can.   ☐ ☐ ☐ ☐ ☐

28. I would enjoy teaching a small child a Bible story or helping a friend understand something from the Bible.   ☐ ☐ ☐ ☐ ☐

29. When I lead a group project, I like to plan so that everyone has a job to do and gets it done.   ☐ ☐ ☐ ☐ ☐

30. I know I have artistic ability and am often able to use it at school or church.   ☐ ☐ ☐ ☐ ☐

31. I can tell when someone is phony or manipulative, even when others don't notice.   ☐ ☐ ☐ ☐ ☐

32. I sometimes notice when people are unkind to another person. After I talk with them, they act kinder or more loving.   ☐ ☐ ☐ ☐ ☐

33. I have had the opportunity to help someone believe in Jesus as his or her Savior.   ☐ ☐ ☐ ☐ ☐

34. I've gone through some difficult situations in my life, but I know God helped me cope.   ☐ ☐ ☐ ☐ ☐

35. I give money or I work for good causes when I see people have a need.   ☐ ☐ ☐ ☐ ☐

	Very Little (1)	Little (2)	Some (3)	Much (4)	Very Much (5)
36. When someone new comes to our school or church, I know I can help them feel comfortable and welcome.	☐	☐	☐	☐	☐
37. I pray for people who ask for prayer because I know that God hears and helps.	☐	☐	☐	☐	☐
38. When there's work to be done or a project to do with a group of people, I enjoy leading the group and helping them finish the project.	☐	☐	☐	☐	☐
39. When someone has a physical problem or is struggling in some way, I enjoy helping them.	☐	☐	☐	☐	☐
40. Sometimes, at school or work or church, I have felt I had to say what I thought the Bible said about certain issues.	☐	☐	☐	☐	☐
41. If a group is working on a project, there are often a lot of details to take care of. I enjoy doing those things for the group.	☐	☐	☐	☐	☐
42. Sometimes when our class is having a discussion, everyone seems confused. At such a time I have said something that helps everyone understand.	☐	☐	☐	☐	☐
43. I would enjoy being in charge of an important activity at school or church in which many jobs have to be done.	☐	☐	☐	☐	☐
44. I know that I could use my artistic or musical or dramatic or writing abilities at school or at church.	☐	☐	☐	☐	☐
45. I can tell when someone is "phony" or pretending to be different than they really are.	☐	☐	☐	☐	☐
46. I believe I am a good listener to friends and classmates who are having a hard time, and I have found Bible verses that have been helpful to me and others.	☐	☐	☐	☐	☐
47. When I know that someone at school or elsewhere is not a Christian, I feel like I would like to help them know Jesus.	☐	☐	☐	☐	☐

	Very Little (1)	Little (2)	Some (3)	Much (4)	Very Much (5)
48. I seem to know when it would be better to pray about a problem than to continue to try to figure it out.	☐	☐	☐	☐	☐
49. If someone needs something that I am able to give him or her, I'm often very willing to help.	☐	☐	☐	☐	☐
50. When new people visit our church school class or school, I know what I can do to help make them comfortable.	☐	☐	☐	☐	☐
51. I know that God listens to my prayers, and I want to help others through my prayers.	☐	☐	☐	☐	☐
52. If given the opportunity, I would enjoy leading a group to get a project done.	☐	☐	☐	☐	☐
53. When I see people who are miserable, I want to find a way to let them know that God and others love them.	☐	☐	☐	☐	☐
54. If given the opportunity, I would like to become a minister or youth pastor or missionary.	☐	☐	☐	☐	☐
55. I like to do things that help other people.	☐	☐	☐	☐	☐
56. I like to help children and classmates understand what the Bible says. I also like to explain things we learn about in school to kids who are having a little trouble.	☐	☐	☐	☐	☐
57. When there are jobs to be done for a group project, I seem to know who could do the work.	☐	☐	☐	☐	☐
58. People have told me that they enjoy my artistic or dramatic or musical or writing or other similar creative abilities.	☐	☐	☐	☐	☐
59. I seem to know if something that is going on—or something someone says—is good or bad.	☐	☐	☐	☐	☐
60. I am happy when other kids come to me for help with a problem of some kind.	☐	☐	☐	☐	☐

	Very Little (1)	Little (2)	Some (3)	Much (4)	Very Much (5)
61. I am able to talk about Jesus to people who don't know him. When I do, they seem to understand.	☐	☐	☐	☐	☐
62. Even when things seem hopeless, I still believe God can do all things.	☐	☐	☐	☐	☐
63. I enjoy helping persons in need by giving of my time or money.	☐	☐	☐	☐	☐
64. I like to invite new kids at school to join me and my friends.	☐	☐	☐	☐	☐
65. I know that I help others when I pray for them because I know God hears my prayers.	☐	☐	☐	☐	☐
66. I know I'm a good leader because I have helped a group at church or school work on a project from start to finish.	☐	☐	☐	☐	☐
67. I know that I have helped some people with problems by spending time with them.	☐	☐	☐	☐	☐
68. I think it's important to talk to others about spiritual things, and I enjoy doing that.	☐	☐	☐	☐	☐
69. I think it's important to do things for others, and I'm happy when I have a chance to do so.	☐	☐	☐	☐	☐
70. When I explain a homework assignment to other kids, I know that I help them because they seem to understand it better when I'm finished.	☐	☐	☐	☐	☐
71. I know when a group project needs better organization to get finished.	☐	☐	☐	☐	☐
72. I think I have a talent for some creative activities.	☐	☐	☐	☐	☐
73. I can usually tell if someone isn't telling the truth.	☐	☐	☐	☐	☐
74. I would be willing to talk to someone going through a hard time.	☐	☐	☐	☐	☐

	Very Little (1)	Little (2)	Some (3)	Much (4)	Very Much (5)

75. I am able to tell when a person doesn't know Jesus Christ, and I feel badly for him or for her. ☐ ☐ ☐ ☐ ☐

76. The Bible says that faith can move mountains. Even though it seems impossible to move mountains, that statement makes some sense to me because I believe God can do anything. ☐ ☐ ☐ ☐ ☐

77. Even though either my parents or I pay for everything we own, I think that everything really comes from God. I feel I should be responsible with what God has given me. ☐ ☐ ☐ ☐ ☐

78. Newcomers at church or school can sometimes be quite different from me and my friends. They may have different interests than I do. They may be from a race or a culture other than my own. That doesn't really bother me. I enjoy trying to make them feel welcome. ☐ ☐ ☐ ☐ ☐

79. I would be very happy if someone asked me to pray for him or her. ☐ ☐ ☐ ☐ ☐

80. I can tell when a group I'm part of is not getting its job done. I'm often the one who wants to do something about it. ☐ ☐ ☐ ☐ ☐

81. I can tell when people feel badly or have problems they're trying to hide. ☐ ☐ ☐ ☐ ☐

82. I think more Christians should speak out on the issues of the day such as abortion, racism, crime, poverty, and so on. ☐ ☐ ☐ ☐ ☐

83. I wish I had more opportunity to help others in the jobs they are doing. ☐ ☐ ☐ ☐ ☐

84. I get excited about discovering new things. I like to tell others about them. ☐ ☐ ☐ ☐ ☐

Session 4
Key Chart

How to Use the Key Chart

STEP 1

Now it's time to transfer your answers from the questionnaire to the key chart.

On the key chart, you'll see in shaded boxes the numbers of the 84 statements. (Notice that they're not all listed consecutively—be careful!)

Behind each statement number, record the answer you gave on the questionnaire. For example, if you answered "Very Much (4)" to question #1 on the questionnaire, write a "4" after the shaded number "1" on the key chart.

STEP 2

After you finish step 1, notice the fourteen spiritual gifts listed down the left side of the page. You've now written six numbers following each gift (*not* counting the shaded numbers).

The three numbers on the left are in the "working gifts" category; the three numbers on the right are in the "waiting gifts" category.

Add the three numbers on the left, and record the sum in the "total" column. Do the same for the three numbers on the right. (*Don't* include the shaded numbers in your total!) Each total should be no higher than 15.

STEP 3

Circle your four highest scores in the "working gifts" category. Write the names of those gifts in Box A at the bottom of the page, starting with the highest score and going to the lowest.

If you have one or more working gifts with the same score, break the tie by adding the scores of the same waiting gifts to the total of your tied working gifts scores. Use the highest scores to decide on the best order for you.

STEP 4

Now circle your four highest gifts in the "waiting gifts" category. If you find that some of your highest scored waiting gifts are the same as some of your highest scored working gifts, use only the waiting gifts that you have not already listed in Box A as working gifts. In Box B, write the names of those waiting gifts.

Key Chart

Spiritual Gift	Working Gifts							Waiting Gifts						
	?	Ans	+	?	Ans	+	?	Ans	= Total	?	Ans	+	?	Ans	+	?	Ans	= Total

Spiritual Gift	?	Ans	+	?	Ans	+	?	Ans	= Total	?	Ans	+	?	Ans	+	?	Ans	= Total
Administration	1	___	+	29	___	+	57	___	=	15	___	+	43	___	+	71	___	=
Creative Ability	2	___	+	30	___	+	58	___	=	16	___	+	44	___	+	72	___	=
Discernment	3	___	+	31	___	+	59	___	=	17	___	+	45	___	+	73	___	=
Encouragement	4	___	+	32	___	+	60	___	=	18	___	+	46	___	+	74	___	=
Evangelism	5	___	+	33	___	+	61	___	=	19	___	+	47	___	+	75	___	=
Faith	6	___	+	34	___	+	62	___	=	20	___	+	48	___	+	76	___	=
Giving	7	___	+	35	___	+	63	___	=	21	___	+	49	___	+	77	___	=
Hospitality	8	___	+	36	___	+	64	___	=	22	___	+	50	___	+	78	___	=
Intercession	9	___	+	37	___	+	65	___	=	23	___	+	51	___	+	79	___	=
Leadership	10	___	+	38	___	+	66	___	=	24	___	+	52	___	+	80	___	=
Mercy	11	___	+	39	___	+	67	___	=	25	___	+	53	___	+	81	___	=
Prophecy	12	___	+	40	___	+	68	___	=	26	___	+	54	___	+	82	___	=
Service	13	___	+	41	___	+	69	___	=	27	___	+	55	___	+	83	___	=
Teaching	14	___	+	42	___	+	70	___	=	28	___	+	56	___	+	84	___	=

Box A: Working Gifts
Highest scored gift: _____
2nd _____
3rd _____
4th _____

Box B: Waiting Gifts
Highest scored gift
not in Box A: _____
2nd _____
3rd _____
4th _____

Session 5
How Do I Use My Gifts for God?

Directions:

1. Find your two top working gifts on these pages.

2. Read what you are good at if you have these gifts. Do all or some of these qualities describe you? How else do you show that you have these gifts? Jot down your thoughts in the space provided.

3. Write down some things you need to avoid when using these gifts. In other words, how might Satan tempt you to misuse these gifts?

Administration

If you have this gift, you are good at

- 👉 organizing ideas, jobs, and people.
- 👉 making plans to get the job done.
- 👉 delegating jobs to others so you don't do all the work.

If you have this gift, be careful not to misuse it by

Creative Ability

If you have this gift, you are good at

- 👉 using your artistic abilities (music, art, writing, drama, dance, etc.) to help others understand more about God.
- 👉 helping others feel closer to God because of what you do.

If you have this gift, be careful not to misuse it by

Discernment

If you have this gift, you are good at

- telling the difference between truth and error, good and evil.
- detecting when someone is manipulative or phony.

_____

_____

If you have this gift, be careful not to misuse it by

_____

_____

_____

Evangelism

If you have this gift, you are good at

- talking about Jesus to those who don't know him.
- leading others to believe in Jesus as their Savior.

_____

_____

If you have this gift, be careful not to misuse it by

_____

_____

_____

Encouragement

If you have this gift, you are good at

- helping people live more Christlike lives because of the kind and affirming things you say.
- comforting, giving good advice, and encouraging those who need help.

_____

_____

If you have this gift, be careful not to misuse it by

_____

_____

_____

Faith

If you have this gift, you are good at

- believing and trusting that God will act in difficult situations.
- inspiring others by your faith and trust in God during difficult times.

_____

_____

If you have this gift, be careful not to misuse it by

_____

_____

_____

_____

Giving

If you have this gift, you are good at

- cheerfully giving of your money or possessions or time to help others.
- assuming responsibility when you see others in need.

_____

_____

If you have this gift, be careful not to misuse it by

_____

_____

_____

Hospitality

If you have this gift, you are good at

- helping strangers or guests feel welcome in an unfamiliar place.
- being kind and courteous to others.

_____

_____

If you have this gift, be careful not to misuse it by

_____

_____

_____

Intercession

If you have this gift, you are good at

- praying faithfully for people who request your prayers.
- praying faithfully for people who haven't requested your prayers but who are in need.
- knowing that you help others because of your prayers.

_____

_____

If you have this gift, be careful not to misuse it by

_____

_____

_____

_____

Leadership

If you have this gift, you are good at

- taking charge of a project or task.
- motivating people to work toward a worthy goal.
- setting a good example for others to follow.

_____

_____

If you have this gift, be careful not to misuse it by

_____

_____

_____

Mercy

If you have this gift, you are good at

- being sympathetic to people who are hurting or in need.
- cheerfully doing kind and helpful things for these people.

_____

_____

If you have this gift, be careful not to misuse it by

_____

_____

_____

Service

If you have this gift, you are good at

- helping others in lots of little ways and enjoying doing this.
- putting the needs of others before your own.

_____

_____

If you have this gift, be careful not to misuse it by

_____

_____

_____

Prophecy

If you have this gift, you are good at

- inspiring people to do God's will.
- taking a biblical stand on social justice issues.
- encouraging others by talking to them about spiritual things.

_____

If you have this gift, be careful not to misuse it by

_____

_____

_____

Teaching

If you have this gift, you are good at

- building good relationships with others.
- explaining things clearly and in an interesting way—especially spiritual things.
- acting as an example for others to follow.

_____

_____

If you have this gift, be careful not to misuse it by

_____

_____

_____

_____

Session 6
Use Those Gifts!

Romans 12:1-13, New Century Version

[1]So, brothers and sisters, since God has shown us great mercy, I beg you to offer your lives as a living sacrifice to him. Your offering must be only for God and pleasing to him, which is the spiritual way for you to worship. [2]Do not change yourselves to be like the people of this world, but be changed within by a new way of thinking. Then you will be able to decide what God wants for you; you will know what is good and pleasing to him and what is perfect. [3]Because God has given me a special gift, I have something to say to everyone among you. Do not think you are better than you are. You must decide what you really are by the amount of faith God has given you. [4]Each one of us has a body with many parts, and these parts all have different uses. [5]In the same way, we are many, but in Christ we are all one body, and each part belongs to all the other parts. [6]We all have different gifts, each of which came because of the grace God gave us. The person who has the gift of prophecy should use that gift in agreement with the faith. [7]Anyone who has the gift of serving should serve. Anyone who has the gift of teaching should teach. [8]Whoever has the gift of encouraging others should encourage. Whoever has the gift of giving to others should give freely. Anyone who has the gift of being a leader should try hard when he leads. Whoever has the gift of showing mercy to others should do so with joy.

[9]Your love must be real. Hate what is evil and hold on to what is good. [10]Love each other like brothers and sisters. Give each other more honor than you want for yourselves. [11]Do not be lazy but work hard, serving the Lord with all your heart. [12]Be joyful because you have hope. Be patient when trouble comes, and pray at all times. [13]Share with God's people who need help. Bring strangers in need into your homes.

1. According to verse 1, our worship of God isn't limited to going to church or doing our devotions. What else could it include?

2. According to verse 2, if we live for God and use our gifts in God's service, what "bonus benefit" will we receive in return?

3. Verses 4-6 bring back the familiar "body" image. Remind yourself of what Paul is teaching us through this picture.

4. What's Paul's main message in verses 6-8? Put it in your own words.

5. In verses 9-13, Paul gives us a big bunch of instructions about the kind of attitude we should have when we use our gifts. Pick one that best describes the way you want to be when you use your gifts and interact with others.

Session 6
My Business Card

My three highest working gifts are

_____   _____   _____

Available for:

_____

_____

_____

Available for:

_____

_____

_____

Available for:

_____

_____

_____

Available for:

_____

_____

_____

Session 6
Certificate of Achievement

This is to certify that

_____
(name)

successfully completed *Discover Your Gifts* for youth on

_____
(date)

at

_____.
(location)

Three "working" spiritual gifts that God has given you

are_____, _____, and _____.

Three "waiting" gifts that God has given you are _____,

_____, and _____.

May you always use all your spiritual gifts to serve others and the Lord.

_____
(teacher)

"Don't let anyone look down on you because you are young, but set an example for the believers in speech, in life, in love, in faith and in purity. . . . Do not neglect your gift, which was given you. . . ."
1 Timothy 4:12, 14a